Americans All biographies are inspiring life stories about people of all races, creeds, and nationalities who have uniquely contributed to the American way of life. Highlights from each person's story develop his contributions in his special field — whether they be in the arts, industry, human rights, education, science and medicine, or sports.

Specific abilities, character, and accomplishments are emphasized. Often despite great odds, these famous people have attained success in their fields through the good use of ability, determination, and hard work. These fast-moving stories of real people will show the way to better understanding of the ingredients necessary for personal success.

Walt Disney

MASTER OF MAKE-BELIEVE

by Elizabeth
Rider Montgomery

illustrated by Vic Mays

GARRARD PUBLISHING COMPANY
CHAMPAIGN, ILLINOIS

For Douglas Small

Picture credits:

Contents

1. Unpaid Paper Boy

One cold winter day in 1910, Mr. Elias Disney said to his family, "I'm going to sell the farm."

Nine-year-old Walt gasped. He loved the apple farm near Marceline, Missouri, where he had lived since he was four. The country was beautiful. Besides, Walt liked to draw the animals—horses, cows, chickens, ducks, and pigs. Drawing was about the only fun he had, because he had so many chores to do.

"Please don't sell the farm!" Walt begged.

His sister Ruth chimed in, "Please, please, Pa!"

Mr. Disney silenced the children with a look. He ruled his household with an iron will and a ready whip. Only three years earlier two of his sons, Ray and Herbert, had run away from home. Walt and seventeen-year-old Roy were now the only boys at home.

"Make some signs for advertising the place," Mr. Disney ordered Roy. "Then you and Walter tack them up on trees and telephone poles."

Walt, hoping for sympathy, looked tearfully at his mother, although he feared it would do no good. Mrs. Disney never went against her husband. The children did not know whether she agreed with Pa or whether she was afraid to speak her mind.

Roy put his arm around Walt and led him out of the room. He always looked out for Walt and treated his younger brother with kindness and understanding. Even the few playthings that Walt and Ruth owned came from Roy, because their father did not believe in "useless" Christmas and birthday gifts.

"Pa has to sell the farm, kid," Roy explained kindly. "The price of apples has dropped so low he can't keep up the mortgage payments. He can't afford hired hands, and he can't run the farm with just you and me to help. Besides, he isn't well."

Early the next summer the Disney family moved to Kansas City, Missouri. With the money from the sale of the farm, Mr. Disney bought a Kansas City *Star* paper route of 2,000 customers. He hired a number of delivery boys at three dollars a week, but he paid his sons nothing for delivering papers twice a day.

"I feed you and clothe you," he reminded them often. "That's enough."

Walt had 50 customers to serve—some in private homes, some in apartment houses. He had to get up at 3:30 A.M. to pick up his papers when the delivery truck dropped off the bundles. There was no time to play with other boys after school because he had to deliver his evening papers before supper.

One cold, snowy morning Roy got up and awakened Walt as usual. Sitting on the side of the bed, trying to tie his shoelaces, Walt fell asleep.

"Come on, kid," Roy said, shaking Walt's shoulder. "You mustn't be late or Pa will beat you." He rumpled Walt's hair fondly.

With a great effort Walt forced his eyes open, finished tying his shoelaces, and followed his brother out into a blinding snowstorm.

As soon as the Disney boys picked up their papers, they separated, each to serve his own customers. With his heavy load, undersized Walt struggled through the snow. In some places the snow was already three feet deep.

Two hours later Walt climbed the icy

steps of an apartment house. Half blind from the snow and cold, he missed a step and fell.

When he finally got inside, the halls of the steam-heated building felt wonderfully warm. Walt climbed flight after flight of stairs and left a newspaper in front of each customer's door. Now he was warm for the first time since crawling out of bed, and he became sleepy.

"I'll lie down on the landing a few minutes," he said to himself. In two seconds he was fast asleep.

When Walt awoke it was broad daylight, and he still had a number of papers in his bag. He hurried to finish his route and then dashed on to school without breakfast. Would there ever be a time, he wondered longingly, when he wouldn't have to carry papers for his father?

2. Under His Father's Thumb

A year went by. Day after day, month after month, Walt delivered newspapers.

When Roy finished high school, he quit working for his father and got a job with pay. Mr. Disney was furious. They had frequent violent quarrels. Finally Roy could no longer bear his father's tyranny.

One evening as Walt was getting ready for bed, his brother said, "I'm leaving, kid."

Walt looked at Roy pleadingly. "Take me with you," he begged.

"No, kid," Roy replied. "You've got to finish school."

"Where are you going?" Walt asked.

"I'll get a job in the harvest fields. I'll leave as soon as Pa is asleep tonight."

Sadly Walt watched his brother's preparations. Roy packed his clothes in a cardboard suitcase. He rolled up a blanket and

put it in his place in bed. If Pa looked in the room, he would think Roy was there, asleep.

Walt wanted to stay awake until his brother left, but the need for sleep was too great. When he awoke at 3:30 the next morning, Roy was gone.

For weeks Mrs. Disney grieved, and so did Walt. After all, his older brother had been his closest friend. Mr. Disney was furious at Roy's leaving home, and he sometimes took his anger out on Walt.

One day Mr. Disney shouted, "You need a whipping, Walter. Go down to the basement."

Although Walt had done nothing wrong, he obeyed. His father followed him.

"I'll teach you to be impudent and disobedient," Mr. Disney raged, raising his strap.

Suddenly Walt grabbed his father's arm and held it.

"Let me go," screamed Mr. Disney. "Let me go, you young rascal!" But Walt did not. For a few minutes the old man struggled, then he gave up and dropped the strap. Walt let go. He knew that his father would never again try to whip him.

The nightmare of delivering newspapers twice a day and the harsh home atmosphere would have made life unbearable for Walt Disney except for two things.

On Saturday mornings, after delivering his papers, Walt took drawing lessons at the Kansas City Art Institute. Stern as Mr. Disney was, he wanted his children to have a good education, and Walt had convinced his father that an education in art was important.

Walt also went to a few movies. A

16

schoolmate's father owned a neighborhood theater. Whenever Walt could convince Pa that the show was "educational," he was allowed to go.

To earn a little money, Walt sold extra newspapers on street corners. He also delivered packages for a drugstore after school before picking up his evening papers. However, the money did Walt no good. Mr. Disney took it from him for "safekeeping."

"You're not old enough to handle money, Walter," Mr. Disney said.

So without telling his father, Walt got a job working noon hours in a candy store across the street from school. At last he had a little money to spend.

One day near the end of 1916, Mr. Disney said, "I've invested your savings, Walter, in a jelly factory in Chicago."

"A jelly factory!" Walt exclaimed. "But I want..."

"It doesn't matter what you want," his father snapped. "I know what's best for you."

In the spring of 1917, about the time the United States entered World War I, Mr. Disney sold his newspaper route and put the money into the jelly factory.

"I'm going to be maintenance chief for the factory," he told the family. "The rest of us will move to Chicago, but Walter will stay here until school is out and help the new owner of the paper route."

Fifteen-year-old Walt grinned happily. For the first time in his life he would be free from his father's control!

3. Ambulance Driver

Instead of joining his family when school let out that summer, Walt got a job. He became a "news butcher" on the Santa Fe railroad, selling candy, cold drinks, and newspapers to train passengers. He made little money, but he enjoyed riding on the trains.

When fall came, Walt's freedom ended. Soon he was in Chicago and back in school. Three evenings a week he took art lessons at the Chicago Academy of Fine Arts. He also studied cartooning by mail.

Again Walt had to work for his father.

He ran the bottle washer and the capper at the jelly factory part-time. Sometimes he acted as night watchman.

The next summer Walt worked at the post office as well as the jelly factory. Sometimes he got a third job at 40 cents an hour on the elevated railroad. He had a special cap for each job. As usual, Mr. Disney insisted on "caring for" his son's money.

Early in the fall Walt got a postcard from Roy: "I've joined the Navy. I'm coming through Chicago. Meet me at the train and we'll have a talk."

Roy looked just the same to Walt. He was the kindest person in the world!

"How are you, kid?" Roy asked, pounding Walt's back affectionately. Walt, tall for his age, grinned down happily at his "big" brother.

"You've grown up," Roy said. "You look as old as some of the fellows in my outfit."

The brothers had little time to exchange news of the past few years. All too soon an officer came along, rounding up the recruits for transportation to the naval training station.

Roy told Walt he'd get in touch and he turned away. Walt gazed after him.

"You there!" snapped the officer. "Time to get aboard." The officer thought Walt was a recruit!

That gave Walt a wonderful idea. If he joined the navy, he could get away from home, something he had wanted to do ever since Roy left!

The navy turned him down. Recruits had to be eighteen, and Walt wouldn't be seventeen until December. So he applied at the Red Cross Ambulance Corps. They agreed to accept him if his parents gave permission.

Mr. Disney refused his permission, but for once Walt stood up to him. "I'm going, Pa, whether you sign for me or not. I'll lie about my age, and I'll run away, like Roy and Ray and Herbert."

To Walt's surprise his mother spoke up. "I'll sign for you, Walter. I'd rather know where you are than have you run away like your brothers."

Although the war ended in November 1918, before Walt's training had been completed, his unit was sent overseas anyway. He spent eleven months in Europe with the Red Cross Ambulance Corps, and he had many interesting experiences. He sent his earnings home to his mother to keep for him.

With arms crossed, Walt poses with a friend in the Red Cross Ambulance Corps. This picture was taken in France.

Walt came home in September 1919. His father wanted him to go back to school and work at the jelly factory, but Walt had other ideas.

"I'm going to be an artist," he said. "I'm going to Kansas City and get a job on the Kansas City *Star*."

Mr. Disney stormed and shouted, but it did no good. Then he tried arguing calmly. Drawing was all right for a hobby, he said, but not for a career.

However, Walt had made up his mind to leave home. He took only enough of his money to live on while he found a job and left the rest, about $500, with his mother.

4. In Business for Himself

Walt did not get a job on the art staff of the *Star* when he arrived in Kansas City in the fall of 1919. But he did find work with the Gray Advertising Company, making sketches for their catalog.

When advertising slowed down, Walt was laid off. Again he turned to the post office for work. From 7:30 A.M. to mid-afternoon he delivered mail. He spent the rest of each day looking for another art job. In the evenings he made up drawing samples.

Just before Christmas Ub Iwerks, a fellow artist at Gray Advertising, came to see Walt. Ub had also been laid off.

After a brief conversation Walt said, "Why don't we go into business together, Ub?"

"Doing what?" asked Ub.

"We could do artwork for any business firm that doesn't have an art staff," Walt replied. "We'd make ads and letterheads —things like that."

Ub nodded thoughtfully. "You're good at cartooning, and I'm pretty good at lettering and airbrush painting. We'd make a real team."

Walt took some of Iwerks' samples and his own and showed them to businessmen who might need artwork. He got several orders. A newspaper publisher agreed to give them desk space in return for free artwork.

Walt wrote to his mother, asking her to send the $500 she was keeping for him. She answered promptly, but she sent no money.

"What do you want it for, Walter?" she asked.

Her letter made Walt angry. He was eighteen now—grown up—and the money belonged to him. Why should his parents treat him as if he were a child?

"I'm going into business," he wrote back. "I need my money for supplies. After all, I earned it. Why shouldn't I decide what to do with it?"

His mother sent only half of his money. It was soon spent on desks, drawing boards, an airbrush, and a tank of air.

The partnership got off to a good start. In its first month of operation it took in $135, and more orders were coming in.

Early in February 1920, Walt saw an ad in the *Star* for a cartoonist at Kansas City Film Ad Company. He called on the firm, hoping to get an order, but they wanted a full-time artist.

"Our company makes one-minute, animated cartoon ads for local theaters," Walt was told. "The job pays $160 a month—full-time work."

Walt wanted the job, but if he took it he would have no time for Iwerks-Disney orders. He went back to the office to talk to Ub.

"It's too good an opportunity to pass up," Iwerks said. "That's more than the two of us together made last month."

The partners decided to separate. Walt would take the position at Kansas City Film Ad, and Ub would take over Iwerks-Disney work.

Two months later Ub telephoned Walt. "Can you get me a job there with you?"

"What about Iwerks-Disney?" Walt asked.

"I'm going broke," Iwerks confessed. "I'm no salesman like you." So Walt got Ub a job at Kansas City Film Ad.

Walt liked his job as a cartoon animator. The art of animation, or making a cartoon seem to move, was very new and very crude. Walt used little figures cut out of paper, with arms and legs fastened so they could be moved. A cutout was photographed in one position with a motion picture camera. Then the arms and legs were moved a trifle and another picture was taken. Again the figure was changed slightly and another picture taken, and so on. When the series of photographs was projected on a screen, the cartoon figure seemed to move.

In his spare time Walt tried to find better ways of making animations. He read all the books he could find on the subject in the public library. His boss lent him an old box movie camera, and night after night Walt worked with it in a neighbor's empty garage. He tried photographing a series of drawings instead of paper cutouts. It took much longer, but

the animated figures were more lifelike.

Soon Walt made a sample reel of cartoon jokes, using drawings in place of cutouts, and sold it to the Newman Theater as a Laugh-O-Gram. The film was so popular that he was asked to make others. Walt decided to leave Kansas City Film Ad and go into business for himself again.

Grudgingly his mother sent him the rest of his money. But it was not enough. He needed thousands of dollars, not hundreds, to start his new business. So Walt visited all the people he had met in Kansas City and tried to get them to invest in his company.

Walt was a good salesman. He soon raised the $15,000 he needed. At not quite 21, Walt Disney became president of the Laugh-O-Gram Corporation. Ub Iwerks was his chief assistant.

5. Failure

In spite of a promising start, the
Laugh-O-Gram Corporation had trouble
making a profit. In less than a year it
went out of business. Walt was left with
nothing but his movie camera and a print
of his latest movie, *Alice in Cartoonland.*
This film was a new idea of Walt's, which
combined animated cartoon figures with
pictures of a live girl.

Walt gave up his apartment and lived
in the Laugh-O-Gram office, sleeping in an
armchair. Often he had nightmares about
delivering newspapers for his father.

He ate one meal a day, in a little Greek restaurant downstairs. Since there was no bathroom in the office, he walked downtown once a week to the Union Station and paid a dime for a tub bath in a public bathroom. He traded artwork for haircuts.

One day Walt got a letter from his brother Roy, now recovering from tuberculosis in a veterans' hospital in Los Angeles.

"I have a hunch, kid," Roy wrote, "that you could use a little dough. I'm enclosing a blank check. Fill it out for any amount up to $30."

Walt used most of the money to pay part of his bill at the Greek restaurant.

Walt tried everything he could think of to make money. He took photographs of news events. He made short movies of babies for parents to show in their living rooms. For the organist of the Isis Theater he made a cartoon that encouraged audiences to join in group singing.

Then a dentist asked Walt to make an animated cartoon that would teach children to care for their teeth. It was to be called *Tommy Tucker's Tooth*.

One evening the dentist telephoned and said, "Your money is ready, the $500 we agreed on. Come on over and get it."

"I can't," Walt replied. "My shoes are at the shoemaker's, and I can't get them until I pay him $1.50."

"Stay right there," the dentist said. "I'll bring the money to you." And he did.

For months Walt kept up this hand-to-mouth life. Once he lived for two days on beans and bread a neighbor gave him. Walt fed the crumbs to the mice that

34

Walt worked to improve animated cartoons with his first movie camera.

gathered in his wastebasket at night. He had become very fond of these little creatures and built cages for them. They kept him from getting lonely.

One mouse in particular seemed extra bright and curious. Walt named him Mortimer. From time to time Walt set Mortimer free on the drawing board and taught him tricks. Walt drew a big circle on a sheet of drawing paper. He taught Mortimer to stay inside that circle, tapping him gently on the nose each time the mouse tried to scamper across the line.

In the summer of 1923 Walt decided to go to California and join Roy, who would soon be getting out of the hospital. He sold his camera to raise the train fare. He packed his few belongings in a cheap suitcase—one shirt, two suits of underwear, some socks, a few drawing materials, and his film of *Alice in Cartoonland*. Then he took the cages with his mice and rode to the end of the streetcar line. In an open field he let the mice go.

Walt turned to leave. After a few steps he looked back. Mortimer sat where Walt had left him. The mouse's eyes seemed very reproachful.

6. Two Partnerships

In July 1923, at the age of 21, Walt Disney arrived in Los Angeles in badly worn jacket and mismatched pants. He had only $40 in his pocket. His prospects did not look bright.

Walt boarded with one of his father's brothers, Robert Disney, paying him five dollars a week. Day after day he walked the streets looking for work. He also wrote to New York movie distributors, trying to interest them in *Alice in Cartoonland*.

One day Walt got a letter that sent him hurrying to the veterans' hospital to see Roy.

"A New York movie distributor, Charles Mintz, wants a series of *Alice* films!" he crowed, sitting on the edge of Roy's bed. "He'll pay $1,500 each! Think of that!"

"How many does he want?" Roy asked.

"Twelve. We'll do it, won't we, Roy? We'll go into business together. With $500 we could make a start, I'm sure of it!"

Roy shook his head. He was due to be discharged from the hospital in a few days, but he had no money except his $85-a-month pension from the government. "Who would lend us $500?"

However, Roy could not long resist Walt's enthusiasm. He soon found himself saying, "Okay, kid. Let's go!"

Roy persuaded Uncle Robert to lend

them $500. Walt went to a neighborhood real estate dealer and asked to rent space for a studio.

"How much can you pay?" the realtor asked.

"About five dollars a month," Walt replied. The man laughed. "We don't need much space," Walt assured him hurriedly. "Just about room enough to swing a cat."

Still laughing, the man agreed to rent the Disneys a cubbyhole in the back of his office for five dollars a month.

Production costs ran higher than Walt had figured. He hired a neighborhood child to pose as "Alice." He worked night and day drawing cartoon figures, and he also built the scenes for the backgrounds. Soon he realized he must have help with the drawings, and he wrote to Ub Iwerks and offered him a job. Ub accepted.

At first Roy did the movie photography, but he could not master the steady cranking rhythm that the old-fashioned hand camera required. So Walt had to hire a real cameraman.

"We've got to raise more money," Roy said one evening as the partners sat down to their usual meal of beans in their little walk-up apartment. "Where can we get it?" Uncle Robert had announced flatly that he would not lend them money again.

"What about that girl Edna you went with in Kansas City?" Walt suggested.

"You leave Edna out of this," Roy snapped. "I'm not going to borrow money from my girl!"

Walt shrugged. "Maybe the organist of the Isis Theater in Kansas City would lend me a few hundred. He liked the animated song sheets I did for him."

Walt wrote to the organist, and he also wrote secretly to Roy's girl, Edna Francis. Both sent some money.

Although Roy was angry because Walt had gone against his wishes, he soon forgave him.

The Disney brothers made one *Alice* film after another, but there was little profit. Walt was always trying to improve the animation and photography, and improvements cost money. He also kept adding to his staff. He took on more artists and began to train them in animation. Then he decided to hire a girl to do stenographic work and also ink the outlines of the pencil drawings and fill them in to make them ready for photographing.

One day while Walt was working, a pretty young girl appeared in the tiny Disney office and applied for a job.

"I'm Lillian Bounds, from Lewiston, Idaho," she told Walt. "I'm staying with my sister, just a few blocks from here."

"Good," Walt said, looking down at her approvingly. "You won't have to pay carfare."

Lillian took the job without bothering to ask what it paid. By the time she learned that her wages were only fifteen dollars a week, she had become so interested in her dynamic, hardworking boss that she stayed on.

Walt and Roy continued to live as cheaply as possible. They paid themselves salaries of $35 a week and put the rest of their income back into the business.

Walt admired Lillian Bounds, but he had no money or time for dates. Instead he would drive her home after they had worked late. When they reached her sister's house, they would sit in the car and talk.

"Come in and meet my sister," Lillian often urged, but Walt always refused. He was ashamed of his clothes—an old sweater and worn-out pants.

One day he asked Roy, the company's

business manager, if he could draw enough money from their account to buy a suit.

Roy grinned. "We'll both buy suits, kid," he replied. "Edna is coming out from Kansas City, and we're getting married."

"That's swell, Roy," Walt exclaimed. "But I guess it means I've got to get a new cook!"

Roy and Edna were married in the spring of 1925. A few nights later Walt was dictating to Lillian in the office. Suddenly he paused. He leaned over and kissed her.

"Which do you think we should pay for first, Lilly, a new car or a ring?" he asked.

"A ring," Lilly replied promptly.

The wedding took place in July 1925, in Lillian's brother's home in Lewiston. Now Walt Disney had a marriage partner as well as a business partner.

46

7. The Lesson Oswald Taught

Lillian quickly learned that life with Walt Disney would never be dull, but it could be uncertain and upsetting.

One day she worked for hours cooking dinner in their apartment kitchen. When dinner time arrived, Walt had not come home. Hour after hour Lillian waited, getting angrier and angrier.

Long after midnight the door opened softly and Walt tiptoed in. Before Lillian could say a word he said, "I'm sorry, Lilly. I forgot about dinner. I was drawing an awfully funny animation scene,

and I didn't realize what time it was."

Lillian laughed helplessly. She just couldn't stay mad at Walt!

The following afternoon Walt came home early. He handed his wife a hatbox tied with a big red ribbon. "Here's a peace offering, Lilly," he said, smiling shyly.

Inside the box was a chow puppy, with another red ribbon around its neck!

Walt loved the puppy as much as Lilly did. He spoiled it with extra food, but he trained it with unlimited patience. Lilly was impressed with Walt's love of animals and his kindness to them.

The first two years of Walt's marriage saw many changes. The business outgrew the real estate office, so Walt leased a store building on Hyperion Avenue and converted it into a studio. He also bought a home near the studio.

After three years *Alice in Cartoonland* began to lose its popularity.

"I've got to think of a new series idea," Walt told Lilly. He began to spend every spare minute sketching different animals. Finally he drew a long-eared rabbit. His entire staff liked it.

"The rabbit can get into all kinds of scrapes," Walt said, "all of them very funny. It should be a good series."

"What will you name him?" Lilly asked. But Walt had not yet decided.

"Write names for the rabbit on slips of paper," Walt directed his staff. "We'll put them in a hat and draw one." "Oswald" was the name that was drawn.

Mintz, the eastern distributor, was delighted with Oswald Rabbit. He sent Walt a contract to sign, which named a price of $2,250 for each Oswald picture.

One day in 1927 Walt said to Lilly, "The Oswald contract will end soon. We'll go to New York, and I will bargain for a new contract personally. I'm going to ask for a raise in fees."

Instead of agreeing to a raise, Mintz told Walt bluntly, "I'll give you $1,800 a reel on a new contract."

Walt protested. "I'm not going to take a cut when Oswald is so popular!"

Mintz smiled unpleasantly. "Oh, yes, you are. If you don't, you lose Oswald entirely, and you also lose your best artists." He explained that he had copyrighted Oswald Rabbit in his own name instead of Disney's, so he owned all legal rights. He also showed Walt the contracts that four Disney artists had signed, agreeing to leave Disney and work for him.

It hurt Walt deeply that employees

whom he had trained would desert him.

"If those men desert me now," Walt said, "they'll leave you in the lurch some day, too."

Mintz only smiled, sure that Walt Disney had no choice but to meet his terms.

However, Walt did not give in. "I can replace those artists easily," he boasted.

Walt wasn't as confident as he sounded. He and Lilly were sad as they packed for their trip home.

"I'll never work for anybody else again," Walt vowed. "Never!"

Before boarding the train, he sent a telegram to his brother: "Everything O.K. Coming home."

"How can you say that?" Lilly protested. "You know it isn't true!"

"I'll make it come true," Walt said.

8. The Birth of Mickey Mouse

On the long train trip across the continent, Walt Disney stared unseeingly out of the coach window. Day after day he tried to think of an animal character around which to build a new cartoon series. His mind went back to his childhood on the farm. He drew cows, horses, chickens, pigs, and geese. None of them satisfied him.

As the train reached the Middle West, Walt exclaimed suddenly, "I've got it!" He began to sketch furiously. Soon he thrust a sheet of drawings into Lilly's hands.

"See what you think of these," he said excitedly.

Lilly looked down at the sketches. She saw a cartoon of a mouse—a merry, appealing little creature. In a way the mouse, with his expressive eyes and his pointed face, resembled Walt. The body of the mouse was pear-shaped. He had pipestem legs in big shoes. He wore two-button pants, a black jacket, and gloves.

"I'll call him Mortimer Mouse," Walt said.

Lilly objected. "That's a horrible name for a character!"

"What's wrong with Mortimer?" Walt demanded. "I called one of my Kansas City mice Mortimer. He was smart. He learned to stay inside a circle on drawing paper. Mortimer learned..."

"I don't care what your Kansas City

mouse learned!" Lilly snapped, her nerves on edge from days of worry and inactivity. "You've got to find a better name for that mouse!"

They argued about it while the train crossed wheat fields, deserts, and mountains. Before it reached the Pacific Coast, they had agreed to call the mouse "Mickey."

"Mickey Mouse is going to make a fortune for us," Walt assured his wife. "He's the kind of a character who can cook up lots of mischief, like a bad little boy. I'll never run out of story ideas for Mickey."

Walt started training new animators immediately, and he set to work on a Mickey Mouse film, *Plane Crazy*. He used farm animals as background and as sources of humor. Animators were sent to zoos and farms to draw animals from life.

The whole Disney staff worked night and day. Lilly and Edna, Roy's wife, helped by tracing the animation drawings on celluloid and inking them so they could be photographed. When *Plane Crazy* was finished, a second Mickey Mouse film was started, and then a third. But nobody would buy them! Something had happened while *Plane Crazy* was being made that changed the whole movie industry!

In October 1927 a "talking picture," *The Jazz Singer*, had been shown. Before that date, movies had been "silent." That is, the actors moved their lips, but they made no sound in the theater. Movie audiences had to read signs flashed on the screen to find out what characters said. In *The Jazz Singer* audiences really heard for the first time what actors on the screen were saying. The picture was

a sensation! After it appeared, owners of movie theaters no longer wanted to show "silent" films.

Walt Disney had spent a great deal of money on his silent Mickey Mouse pictures. Now they seemed worthless.

"What are we going to do with these films?" Roy asked at last, very discouraged.

"We'll make them over," Walt said. "We'll add sound to the film."

Roy stared at his brother. "That's impossible," he said.

"I'll find a way," Walt insisted. "Sound will make our pictures much better." He began to experiment with sound in the third Mickey Mouse film, which he called *Steamboat Willie.*

Lean months followed. It took time and money to solve the problems of adding

Mickey Mouse, top, is shown in *Steamboat Willie,* Walt's first sound cartoon. Below is Minnie Mouse in an early cartoon.

sound to a film. And when it was accomplished at last, the brothers ran into more trouble. Distributors wanted to buy the Disney films outright.

Walt refused. "Nobody is ever going to own any of our pictures again," he said stubbornly, remembering Oswald Rabbit. "We'll rent our films, we won't sell them."

Although the Disney Studio needed money badly, Roy stood by his brother. The Disneys distributed their own movies.

To add to Walt's troubles, Ub Iwerks left him to set up his own shop. To Walt, this desertion was sheer treason. He couldn't bear to talk about it.

Walt drove his staff unmercifully. Every detail of every picture had to be perfect, no matter how many times each drawing had to be done over. He drove himself even harder than he did his staff. Often he worked up to fourteen hours a day.

"I have a little work to finish," he told Lilly one evening after dinner.

Lilly went with him to the studio. She stretched out on the sofa and watched her husband working at his drawing board. Soon she drifted off to sleep. The next thing she knew Walt was bending over her, shaking her gently.

"What time is it?" Lilly asked sleepily.

"Ten-thirty," Walt replied, glad that she didn't have a watch. He drove her home and somehow managed to keep her from seeing a clock before she went to bed. It was 2:30 in the morning!

The first Mickey Mouse film opened in New York in September 1928. Mickey Mouse, using Walt Disney's voice, quickly became a star. Audiences laughed at Mickey and loved him.

9. Fame

Walt could not enjoy his success. He had worked too hard too long. He became cross and irritable. He shouted at his staff, at Roy and Edna, and even at Lilly, whom he adored. Finally he went to a doctor.

"You need a long rest," the doctor told Walt. "Drop everything and get away from the studio. Take a trip, and when you come back stop working such long hours. Find yourself some hobbies. Otherwise your health will fail again."

Walt followed the doctor's orders. During several months of leisurely travel he regained his health, his cheerful disposition, and his zest for living.

Soon after he returned from his vacation, Walt learned about a process for color photography.

"That's what I've been waiting for," he exclaimed. "We'll scrap *Flowers and Trees* and reshoot the whole thing in color."

"We've already finished half of that picture in black and white!" Roy protested.

"*Flowers and Trees* is a natural for color photography," Walt insisted.

"But think how much more color photography will cost!" Roy exclaimed.

"Oh, you'll find some way to raise the money," Walt replied cheerfully.

They quarreled about it, but Walt would not give in. Roy finally raised the necessary money, and Walt rushed into color production of *Flowers and Trees*.

However, he took time out to buy a peace pipe and place it on his brother's desk. Roy hung the pipe on the wall of his office.

When *Flowers and Trees* was finished, Roy admitted that Walt had been right to gamble on color. The picture won a Motion Picture Academy Award as the best cartoon of 1931, and again the Disney Studio led all of its competitors.

Walt continued to search for perfection. He constantly looked for ways to improve animated cartoons. One day he stopped in to see Webb Smith in the Disney story department. Webb's office wall was covered with a series of sketches that told the story of the picture then in progress.

"I just had these offices redecorated, Webb," Walt complained. "You're ruining the wall with those thumbtacks."

Donald Duck has always delighted fans. Here Donald plays three roles.

"Sorry, Walt," Webb replied. "I didn't think of that."

Walt stopped frowning at the offending thumbtacks and studied Webb's sketches.

"Um," he murmured thoughtfully. "You can follow the story from these sketches better than from a written outline."

The next day a truckload of corkboard was delivered to the Disney Studio, and a

65

permanent storyboard was installed in each office of the story department.

In the early 1930s the Great Depression swept over the nation. More than 18 million people were out of work. Disney Studio, however, continued to prosper. In five years Walt's staff increased from 150 employees to more than 750. The studio on Hyperion Avenue was enlarged, and

A messenger delivers congratulations and flowers to Walt on Mickey's birthday.

Walt started a training class for cartoon artists.

During these years Walt Disney made many cartoon shorts. He made Donald Duck pictures, Silly Symphonies, *The Tortoise and the Hare*, and *The Three Little Pigs*. These were all very popular.

Still Mickey Mouse was Walt's best known character. He had become more than a movie star. He was seen everywhere—on school tablets, watches, toys, and children's clothes. There was also a Mickey Mouse comic strip, printed in 1,000 newspapers, and there were hundreds of Mickey Mouse Clubs in 40 different countries. In 1935 the League of Nations presented a medal to Walt Disney, calling Mickey Mouse "a symbol of international good will." Walt and his cartoon characters had become world famous.

10. "Disney's Folly"

One day in 1935 Walt said, "I'm going to make a full-length cartoon movie of *Snow White and the Seven Dwarfs.*"

Lilly protested. "Dwarfs aren't very nice, Walt."

"*My* dwarfs will be," Walt assured her. "Each one is going to have a special personality. One will be the bossy type. One will be cross and grumpy, and another cheerful and happy. One will be bashful, another sleepy, and another sort of dopey."

"But cartoons are for short films, kid,"

Roy objected. "Nobody will sit through a long cartoon."

Walt would not listen. Soon word spread through the studio—and through Hollywood—that Walt Disney was about to make a big mistake. People called his new project "Disney's Folly."

Walt paid no attention. He picked a small, select group of artists and technicians and gave them an office adjoining his own, where he could keep an eye on what they were doing.

Ub Iwerks, who had left Walt some years before to start his own film company, was rehired to work with the *Snow White* crew. Even though Walt had been unhappy at Ub's earlier decision to strike out for himself, he refused to let anything stand in the way of making *Snow White* a successful film.

Walt soon learned he needed twice the money he had originally figured *Snow White* would cost.

"We'll never get our money back out of this picture," Roy grumbled.

"We certainly won't," Walt retorted, "unless I can keep it up to Disney standards, and I can't do that without money."

"I suppose you want me to borrow some more," Roy said wearily.

"Yes," Walt agreed. "I figure I'll need about $250,000."

Roy whistled. "A quarter of a million dollars! Well, I'll do my best, but don't count on it."

The next day Roy reported, "The bank's vice-president wants to see this picture, *Snow White and the Seven Dwarfs*."

"He can't!" Walt protested. "It isn't half finished."

"If you want that money," Roy replied shortly, "you'd better show Mr. Rosenberg what you've done."

Walt hated to show anybody an unfinished film. However, this time he had to do it. He pieced out finished color film with black and white, and even with rough pencil sketches.

One morning Walt sat in a projection room beside Mr. Rosenberg as the hodgepodge which was to be *Snow White and the Seven Dwarfs* was shown on the screen. Walt kept up a running explanation. He became more and more desperate as the hours wore on. He took the part of each character in turn, trying to make his voice sweet and girlish like Snow White's, harsh and cruel like the stepmother's, or squeaky like a dwarf's.

Mr. Rosenberg sat and watched, wooden-faced. By the time the session ended, Walt was sure the loan would be refused.

Still silent, Mr. Rosenberg got in his car and started the engine. Then he said, "That thing is going to make a hatful of money."

Walt felt weak with relief.

Snow White did make a lot of money. It quickly became the most popular cartoon movie that had ever been made. Some of its songs, "Whistle While You Work," "Heigh-Ho," and "Some Day My Prince Will Come," became nationwide hits. Dwarf toys sold by the million. A factory, working around the clock, couldn't keep up with the demand for Sneezy, Bashful, Dopey, Sleepy, Doc, Grumpy, and Happy.

Lilly, Roy, Walt's staff, and all of his competitors were amazed at the popular-

The seven dwarfs appealed to all who saw them in Walt's full-length cartoon.

ity of *Snow White*. Walt was not. He had been sure all the time that people would like it.

When Walt and Roy repaid the bank loan, they decided to borrow more money and build a huge, new, modern studio in Burbank near Los Angeles.

Their bankers had been delighted with the success of *Snow White and the Seven*

Dwarfs, but they were not convinced that future Disney films would be equally profitable.

"Build your studio so that it can be made into a hospital if your business fails," the bankers said. "Then we'll okay the loan."

During the building of the new studio, the Disney brothers' parents moved to California to live. Since leaving home, Walt had had little to do with any of his family except Roy. Now, however, he welcomed the chance to show his father how successful he was, and he took him on a tour of the unfinished studio. He explained what each building was for, how it would be furnished, and what it would cost. He proudly displayed his suite of offices on the top floor.

"It will all be air-conditioned," he

boasted. "You can get any kind of weather you want, any time."

His father listened in silence to Walt's enthusiastic description. Finally he asked, "What can it be used for, Walter?"

Walt raised his expressive eyebrows. "Why, it will be a studio! This is where I'll work. I'm a big executive now, you know."

"I mean," said his father, "what can the building be used for if somebody else takes it over?"

Walt grinned wryly. So his father, like his bankers, thought he might fail!

"It can be used as a hospital," he replied shortly.

11. The Troubled Years

In 1940 the Disneys moved from the old studio on Hyperion Avenue to the new one in Burbank. They now had 1,500 employees. Walt's training class numbered 100 students.

Disney Studio was the undisputed leader of the cartoon movie industry, envied by all its competitors. Walt Disney was on top of the world. Yet he still had nightmares about his paperboy years!

Walt had always tried to make his studio a good place to work. He provided the best possible equipment and supplies. Employees were asked to call him by his first name. Walt wanted his staff to be happy. He wanted his studio to have a warm, friendly atmosphere.

Nevertheless, his employees grew unhappy and in 1941 they went on strike. Never again did Walt feel the same toward his workers. After the strike was settled, he grew more and more aloof.

Walt had made no intimate friends. He did not allow anyone except his wife and his brother Roy to get very close to him. Over the years Walt had devoted so much time and thought to his work that there had been little leisure to develop friendships.

However, Walt never allowed himself

to get too busy for family life. He had
two daughters now, Diane, born in 1933,
and Sharon, born in 1936. Both of the
girls adored their father, and he them.
Walt gave his daughters all the love and
understanding he had missed in his own
childhood. He was never too busy to
listen to any of their problems, to attend
father-daughter dinners, or take the girls
to zoos or amusement parks.

One day they went to the pier in Santa

Monica. The rides were the usual whirligig, ferris wheel, and roller coaster types. There was nothing interesting or really different about them.

"Amusement park designers seem to think that all the customers want is thrills," Walt complained, as he followed his daughters off of an airplane tumbling ride. "Why can't they appeal to the imagination and to a love of beauty, too?"

"Come on, Daddy," cried Diane, tugging his hand. "Let's go on the bumping cars."

"Yes, let's," Sharon piped up.

Walt grumbled, but his eyes twinkled. "Bump, thump, thump! That's all there is to the thing." Still, he grinned down at the girls and let them pull him toward the bumping car concession.

"Watch out!" Walt warned suddenly. "Don't step in that melting ice cream on the walk. And don't touch those dirty, smeary railings."

While his daughters jumped up and down in excitement, Walt bought the tickets. He wondered why an amusement park couldn't be kept clean. Why couldn't the managers have a staff to clean up constantly after the customers?

As Walt Disney settled himself on the seat of the tiny car with a small girl on either side, he made a vow. "Some day I'm going to build an amusement park— a clean one—with interesting, imaginative rides. It will be a place that parents as well as children will enjoy."

The Disney girls had no idea how famous their father was. The family lived quietly and had little social life. They usually went to bed at nine o'clock, unless Walt worked late. Walt and Lilly enjoyed their home, their daughters, and each other. The girls heard their parents argue only when animal pests raided Lilly's prized garden. Walt would not allow any traps or poisons on the place.

"Squirrels and rabbits have a right to eat, too," he would say. "You can go to the store, Lilly, and buy strawberries, but they can't."

When Diane started to school, she learned how important her father was. One evening when Walt came home from the studio, she looked up at him, wide-eyed.

"Daddy," she asked, "are you *the* Walt Disney?"

Walt grinned shyly. "Why, yes, I guess I am."

"Please give me your autograph, Daddy," said Diane.

12. New Projects

World War II brought Walt Disney's current projects to a halt. When the war ended, he resumed work on three cartoon features, *Cinderella*, *Alice in Wonderland*, and *Peter Pan*. He also began to make other movies besides cartoons.

On a visit to Alaska, Walt went into a little camera shop run by photographer Al Milotte and his wife Edna.

"How would you like to make some pictures for me?" he asked.

The Milottes looked at each other doubtfully. "What kind of pictures?" Al inquired.

Walt raised his eyebrows. "Oh, pictures

of Alaska...mining...fishing...Eskimos...
wildlife." The Milottes finally agreed to
try it.

None of their first pictures pleased Walt.
Then Al Milotte suggested photographing
the life of fur seals on the Pribilof Islands
off the coast of Alaska.

Cinderella chats with her friends—a mouse
and two birds—in her attic bedroom.

Immediately Walt wired back: "SHOOT FUR SEALS."

For a year Al Milotte lived with Eskimos and photographed seals. Each time he sent a batch of developed film to Walt, he received a wire saying, "MORE SEALS."

Eventually Walt Disney made a 30-minute picture out of the miles of film Milotte had sent him. He called it *Seal Island*. It won an Academy Award for the best two-reel short subject in 1948. So Walt made more True Life Adventures.

Then he began to make movies using real actors instead of cartoon characters. *Treasure Island* was the first, in 1949. *The Story of Robin Hood*, *Rob Roy*, and *The Sword and the Rose* followed.

During these years Walt took up a wonderful hobby: railroading. He had been

84

fascinated by trains ever since that summer he had worked as a "news butcher." Now he decided to build a model train. It would be no tiny toy to run on a table or around the floor of a room. His train would be big enough to ride in, a real railroad at one-eighth scale.

Under the direction of the machine-shop foreman of Disney Studio, Walt began building a locomotive. Every day he took an hour or two off to work in the shop. He spent most of his Saturdays there and many evenings as well.

At the time the Disney family was planning to build a fine new house. One day Walt came home with a legal document. "I want you to sign this," he told his wife and daughters.

"What is it, Daddy?" asked Sharon, who was now a teen-ager.

"It's a right-of-way contract," Walt explained. "It will give me the right to put railroad tracks on the grounds of our new house. And that includes a tunnel."

Lilly and her daughters laughed at the idea of a tunnel underneath their new home, but Walt was serious.

"Sign," he said, "or we don't build the house."

Lilly sobered. "Railroad tracks would cost thousands of dollars, Walt. They would lower the value of the property, because not every buyer would want a yard full of track."

Walt shook his head. "We'll never sell."

"Oh, yes, we will," his wife replied. "When the girls marry, we won't want such a big house. Build your tracks on the studio grounds, please, Walt!"

Walt refused. "Sign," he commanded.

Again Lilly looked at her daughters. Then she picked up a pen. Before she could sign her name, Walt smiled and put the contract in his pocket. "I'll trust you, Lilly," he said. "I just wanted to know you'd do it."

It took Walt a year and a half to build the locomotive and the boxcars, flatcars, and caboose to go with it. Everything was made to scale and everything worked.

Walt thoroughly enjoyed his miniature train. He liked to wear an engineer's cap and carry a railroader's long-spouted oil-can around with him. Each car would hold one passenger. Every visitor to the Disney home was invited to ride on the train, even women wearing long evening dresses.

13. Walt's "Magic Kingdom"

In the early 1950s Walt Disney decided
to carry out his dream of building a clean,
imaginative amusement park. His own
children were grown up now, but his
grandchildren could enjoy it, and so could
all the other children in the world.

"You really want to build an *amusement park*?" Roy asked. "What a screwy idea!" He refused to let Walt have the money he wanted for the project.

So Walt borrowed on his life insurance and bought 160 acres of land near Anaheim, about 25 miles from Los Angeles. He planned to call his playground Disneyland. However, Walt needed a lot more money before he could begin to build. Where could he get it?

One day Walt had a great idea. Television was new and was becoming quite popular. Why not go on television? A weekly television show would provide money with which to build Disneyland and would also be wonderful advertising.

Walt's plan worked. His television show, *Disneyland*, was an instant hit and, when his amusement park opened in 1955, it was unbelievably popular. Millions of visitors, young and old, flocked to see it. They came from every state in the Union and from many foreign countries.

Walt was often asked if the tremendous success of Disneyland surprised him.

Visitors to Disneyland spin around in huge teacups on this imaginative ride.

"Why, no," he replied. "I believed in it. I knew people would like it."

No baby ever got more loving care and attention from its parents than Disneyland got from Walt. He often walked about the grounds, leaving notes on blue paper for workers who failed to keep their area clean or for those who were not kind and cheerful to the "guests." At least twice a week he flew over Disneyland to check it from the air.

Walt never stopped working on Disneyland. It was his "Magic Kingdom." Each season he added more and more attractions. Every year he had everything in the park freshly painted.

One day someone suggested that Walt Disney should run for mayor of Los Angeles. Walt lifted his eyebrows and shook his head.

"Why should I want to be mayor?" he asked. "I'm already king."

In 1966 Walt Disney was undoubtedly the best-known and best-loved person in the United States. His pictures had brought great pleasure to children. An entire generation had grown up on his movies. To millions of Americans the name "Walt Disney" on a picture meant good, clean entertainment. Of the hundreds of movies Walt made, there wasn't one that he would not want his own family to see.

Walt had received so many awards that he needed an entire room to display them. There were more than 30 Motion Picture Academy Awards, and almost 700 other honors. There were decorations from foreign governments, honorary degrees from colleges, medals and trophies from various organizations.

Of all his honors Walt's favorite was the first Oscar he had received. The Motion Picture Academy had presented it to him many years earlier for creating Mickey Mouse. It was natural for Walt to prefer this trophy. After all, on the mouse he had built his kingdom, the Wonderful World of Walt Disney.

Late in 1966 Walt Disney needed an operation, and he entered the hospital that had been built across the street from his Burbank studio. On December 15, at the age of 65, he died.

Many people thought that Walt Disney Productions would fail now that its guiding genius was gone. Walt had pioneered animation. Most of the techniques now used by other cartoon moviemakers had been his own ideas. He had built up Walt Disney Productions from a tiny company operating from a hole-in-the-wall to a rich and powerful corporation. Even Roy, who had always handled the finances, freely admitted that Walt had made the company what it was. It had been Walt's talent and imagination, his vision, his confidence, his stick-to-itiveness, his willingness to take risks that had made the company famous and successful. Walt *was* Walt Disney Productions.

Now the world's greatest master of make-believe was dead. However, his company did not go to pieces. Led by Walt's brother Roy, who for years had been president of Walt Disney Productions, the studio continued on the course Walt Disney had set. It kept on making wholesome, entertaining movies, and Disneyland continued to delight young and old from all over the world.

Index